WHERE SHADOWS CHASE THE LIGHT

WHERE
SHADOWS
CHASE THE
LIGHT

A collection of poetry and illuminations

RON SHAW

First Edition: April 2025

ISBN 979-8-9891240-8-4 (Paperback)
ISBN 979-8-9891240-9-1 (Hardcover)
ISBN 979-8-9925387-1-7 (Ebook)
ISBN 979-8-9925387-0-0 (Audiobook)
LCCN: 2025902079

10 9 8 7 6 5 4 3 2 1

Editor: Ron Shaw
Cover Design & Interior Layout: Danna Mathias Steele

Published by Evocative Impressions, LLC

Evocative Impressions, LLC
P.O. Box 6, Sandown, NH 03873
evocativeimpressions.com

Table of Contents

Foreword

Welcome to *Where Shadows Chase the Light*, a collection spanning over 20 years of my life. These poems and fragments are the result of countless moments—both the soaring highs and the crushing lows—that life has gifted me. They are born from experience, crafted in reflection, and shared here as a testament to the emotions that have shaped me.

My poetry is an exploration of contrasts: the shadows that speak to our fears and the light that offers solace and clarity. Through free verse, I've sought to capture the unfiltered essence of these moments—raw, unpolished, and deeply human. These words are not just stories; they are glimpses of my heart, a way of embracing the love, pain, hope, and despair that have accompanied me on this journey.

This collection is both deeply personal and universal. It is my love letter to the feelings that have carried me, and my offering to you—an invitation to walk through the darkness and the light as I have. I hope that in these pages, you will find reflections of your own experiences and moments that resonate in ways both profound and unexpected.

Thank you for joining me in this exploration. Let us step together into these shadows and light, and discover what waits within.

—Ron Shaw

PART 1

Breaths on the Edge of Dawn

Indulgence

Bodies in motion,
twisting, turning,
sweat dripping from our skin.

Sheets falling from the bed,
ravenous moans of ecstasy,
breaking the silence of the night.

Every touch–precise,
each embrace–divine,
pushing, pulling,
in all directions.

The world stands still,
yet, our bodies defy it.
Never have flames danced
so passionately upon the snow.

And We Walked

We walked together in the spring,
the air, crisp, upon our backs,
new songs of birds,
sounding sweeter with the years,
life blooming all around us,
flowers on every bush and tree.

We walked together in the summer,
the warm sunlight on our faces,
the music of thunder,
with lightning on the chase.
Crickets chirping in the darkness
reminded us of childhood dreams.

We walked together in the autumn,
leaves crunching beneath our feet,
children running for the school bus,
joyful parents we would meet.
Alas, the trees fall barren
as the season changes again.

I did not walk with you this winter;
your time to walk with me was gone.
You had returned to your father
in the house of the Lord.
Now you walk with many others
with whom you walked before.

And someday,
when my new spring begins,
we shall walk together once more.

Life in Stone

My life is like a stone,
and I, the stonemason.
I received it with its rough
and jagged exterior,
left by the Creator
for me to examine and reshape.

Slowly, through the years,
I notice rough spots
have become smooth.
Though in this world
it shall not obtain perfection;
that, shall not come
until the Creator calls me home.

My Thanks to You

To you,
I give my humble thanks
for the trees
and air to breathe.

To you,
I give my adoring admiration
for the gift of life,
a grace given to me.

To you,
I give my heart and soul,
for when all is lost,
you shall guide me home.

Winter Warm

The branches hang heavy with snow,
the wind moving the drifts to and fro.
I cleared a path for us,
to bring us out into the open.

Under the light of the moon,
and the twinkle of the stars,
let's dance and hold one another close.
Let the love in our hearts
warm us on this cold winter night.

A Chapter

In poems, there are words.
In songs, there is music.
In love, there are hearts.
And in the end,
you have been part of my story.

Sweetest Songs

There are songs for joy and pain,
songs for sun and rain,
songs to celebrate and mourn.

But the sweetest songs,
however, always remind me of you.

Threaded Time

Slowly, souls are entwined,
fate twisting and weaving them together.
Even beyond this life,
they are not to be separated.

In Perfect Time

Blue skies of morning,
rolling hills of green grass,
willows swaying on the gentle breeze,
sunlight reflecting off the pond.

A city in motion—
traffic up and down the avenue,
each person walking forward
to some predetermined destination.

Building lights dance
to a magical symphony,
just feeling the emotion of the music
makes me feel better.

I cannot control the music—
I don't need to.
It moves me in perfect time,
telling me its story.

At times, it lifts me
higher and higher.
At others, it digs
into the darkness within me.

Move me, guide me,
let the words flow out.

One Last Embrace

Can I see you just one last time?
Can you wrap your arms around me,
one final embrace.

Let me taste your salty-sweet lips again,
moved to emotion by loneliness.
Adding new pictures to the wall—
filling the voided spaces of my life.

The tender flesh beneath my hands,
her soft, silky hair on my chest.
In sweet bliss, my soul expands,
a fleeting moment, my very best.

Lost and found,
found and lost—
none of it simpler than the first.

Send me back home;
do not let me be vanquished here.
Time slips like shadows across my soul—
there is no room to breathe.

Tomorrow Awaits

Sunday morning,
church bells ringing.
Pews are all bare—
the preacher man stands before the altar,
palms raised to the air.

Though mortal words
may not be heard,
his prayers ascend
beyond this world
to a heaven that awaits.

What places we have gone,
or to those we shall go,
waste not a moment on despair,
for time fades just so.

We have come to this place,
so have we been in this time.
Let not the fear of darkness take you,
as tomorrow's sun shall soon rise.

New Wings

Fly away, up to the stars—
free yourself from all that you are.
Feel your life as though
you had never known life before.

Sift through your sadness,
sort it out on the shelves.
If the weight is too much,
reach out and call for someone else.

Struggles are never easy;
a fighter always has a chance.
When it all comes crashing down,
turn around and take a second glance.

Someday soon, you will come to realize
that reliance on fate
will leave you struggling
to try and survive.

Fly away into the sunset—
it's time for you to be free.
Someday, I know you'll come home
on a warm summer breeze.

Do as you must to figure out
what will be your plan.
Take the long road home—
it gives you more time to understand.

Take my one-way ticket,
fly to where you can.
Find a deserted island,
bury your troubles under the sand.

Fly away into the cold dark night,
but know that I'll be there
when you can no longer
take to flight.

I'll lift your head,
carry you home,
then continue your flight
as if it were my own.

Hang on to me—
don't let the fear drag you in.
Just reach out your arms,
and I'll pull you back again.

Goodnight for now;
I'll see you as the sun rises.
Your dreams for tomorrow
shall reveal their disguises.

East of Dawn

Rise to the north,
fall to the west.
When the heavens depart to the south,
there shall be a new dawn in the east

Into the Sun

Softly spoken like the wind,
days go by, and I am stuck here again.
No progression on this path—
I must have fallen off.

Pick me up and carry on;
the day is too short,
the night too long.

Just another moment of clarity—
tomorrow I'll be gone,
but today is just for me.

Have you seen me in the sullen night?
I walk in my dreams,
walking into the dead of night.

I am just a shadow where they stand.
So tomorrow, when it comes,
I will again follow the movement
of the Puppet Master's hand.

There is only one simple request I must make:
guide me as we walk into the sun,
for surely, in the end,
to the grave we must all take.

PART 2

Murmurs of Longing

Too Young

Too young is this love
for it to be dying away.
Too young is this love
for us to have forgotten all it has taught.

Too young is this love
to have been damaged beyond repair.
Too young is this love
that the sweet taste of your lips still rests on mine.

Too young is this love
there is so much more for us to enjoy.
Too young is this love
that boundaries we've never seen still have a way around.

Too young is this love
for one to hold another down.
Too young is this love
for all things once felt to have changed.

But, my dear, we are too young,
and every day shall reveal a new page.

Soul Bound

When the stars shine bright
in the heavens up above,
let yourself drift away.

We are only bound to this earth
when that's all we allow ourselves to believe.

The world out there holds many hidden doors,
and if for a moment you let go,
you'll find your soul
cannot be bound.

Innocence

Somewhere off in the distance,
I hear a foghorn blow.
It makes me dream of days gone by,
and I remember
how youthful innocence had once been.

Such a pleasant state—
to be ignorant and naïve to this world.
But with age,
we are doomed, it seems,
to become aware of the unpleasant things in life.

Forbidden Allure

That which is forbidden
never tasted so sweet.
For he would move heaven and earth for her—
the words need only be said.

When it comes to the love that is felt,
no task would be impossible.

Shall it be that I want a lifetime or more?
It is done.
Shall I remain only a safe place in the sun?
It is done.

Twist of Passion

It happened once or twice;
I wish I could say it had been more.
Caught up in the moment,
feeling the world move as it had never before.

Each kiss seemed passionate,
each touch soft and sweet,
lost in the moment,
swept off my feet.

Two bodies connecting close inside
make even the strongest person quiver,
leaving nothing left to hide.

Souls uniting in a passionate twist,
and it all began
with this earth-moving kiss.

Pull and Release

You are my muse,
my soul's inspiration.
You drive me to the edge of insanity,
then reach out as though to pull me in.

And yet, with such elegance and grace,
you retract your arm,
and I fall upon my face.

But still, in the madness of the summer night,
I run back to you.
Because you are my inspiration—
the drive to feed my need.

A Moment

A moment to love,
a moment to breathe—
a moment with you is all I need.

A moment in time,
a moment to hide—
a moment without you feels so empty inside.

Last Hours

Woe to my friend—
parting comes too soon.
What wickedness it is to see
the fall taken so fast.

How the years have passed,
arriving us at this moment
with nothing left but these—
these fading last hours.

'Tis the cruelty of life,
this game of death it plays.
How shall we recount the times
with such a short span to come?

But alas, we shall be reborn,
without suffering or pain,
unto a new day, a new beginning.

As we seek comfort with loss,
it seems time shall be
both friend and foe.

Softness of Goodbye

Now that you're gone,
I'm not quite sure what to say.
You were always there
to help me make it through another day.

I can tell you I will miss you,
but that really doesn't do much now.
It's so hard to believe
that you are somewhere out beyond the clouds.

If I ever break down and cry,
please don't worry about me.
It's hard to take this loss
without clearing my eyes to see.

So tonight, I shall send you
a heart that could once love.
I know someday we will meet again,
somewhere far above.

May your eyes rest softly tonight
and bless all that you love.

Sweet Angel

Don't you cry, sweet angel,
don't you cry tonight.
I never said I don't love you—
I tried with all my might.

Every day gets harder
on this broken road.
I can't wait to tell you, baby,
I'm coming home.

I've got to keep on dreaming—
it's just the way I am.
Can't make many more changes
just to be a better man.

Wipe away those tears;
time will pass us by.
Someday I'll get to tell you,
this time I'm coming home.

We've done all we can to make this,
but it fell into the ground.
Been waiting for tomorrow,
not taking time to look at the past.

What Remains

When all is forgotten,
when my body fades away,
when my tomorrow ends with today,
when my eyes discover the light
one last time—

when all was forgotten,
your love was all that remained.

All of It

Do you feel for me anymore?
The shadows grow longer, creeping closer,
and I can't feel it anymore.
What I feel is it dying—
all of it!

You drift like a phantom,
while I am stuck here waiting,
waiting to see
what awaits me next.

PART 3:

Labyrinth of Shadows

Reborn to the Night

Do not follow me,
this is not the way you want to go.
The road here has been tampered with.
It will only misdirect you from what you already know.

Do not take my lead,
I have warned thee.
Blood shall be spilt,
if you take direction from me.

Look back towards the east,
as the new sun rises above the darkened night.
Do not try to save me.
I have chosen my way, as must you.

Follow not the heavenly glare
of her mystic moon.
Look towards the east, child,
and let the sun lead you home.

I have been reborn to the night,
and it comforts me.
I no longer live
in your world of hatred and crime.

We are now free,
to wander beneath an endless sky.

Lake of Fire

The ancient eagle cries as it flies above the lake of fire.
It has led you here to feed its empty desire.
Step on the shore, but I caution you: beware.
This lake may look so soothing through the layman's glare.

The waves shimmer, oh, so soothing—a dreamer's spell,
but touch the crest, and you'll taste the edge of hell.
It whispers to you—come closer, closer still.
The voices hum like ghosts on the wind, bending your will.

They call your name, those ancient chants,
repeating the rhythm of your dark romance.
They sing, "Forgiveness waits where the fire churns,"
but the heat pulls deeper, and the fire burns.

Do not let this be your last journey, dear friend.
Hear not the lies it speaks of the world's end.
Still, you sit and ponder the choices you've made.
Slowly, it consumes you, like a mantis upon its prey.

Do you hear me? Or has the succubus won?
Her gaze devours; the spell is undone.
The serpent waits, its coils so tight,
turning your flesh to violet, then fading to white.

And with its glistening scales, it draws you near,
dragged into flames, the echo of fear.
This is the reign, the reign of fire and pain,
where shadows writhe in hell's fiery rain.

Give In

Give in to your pain,
so you will feel it no more.
Give in to your pain,
as you have done so many times before.

Give in to your pain,
so you may taste life again.
Give in to your pain,
let your pain win.

Give in to your pain,
I will show you the road home.
Give in to your pain,
for while you hold onto this pain,
you shall always be alone.

Your Day

Today is the day you were born,
but not the day that you chose.
The moon rose high in the amethyst sky;
you were forced from the womb through a hose.

Today is the day you were born,
to a world of heartache and pain.
Your mother wanted to love you;
your father could not feel the same.

Today is the day you were born,
never given the proper clothes.
You were laid to rest beneath your mother's chest,
as tears ran down her nose.

Today is the day you were born,
not to a king or a queen.
Born to the night, a child of sight—
only the world could fear what you dream.

Today is the day you were born.
It was also the day that you died.
Now that it's all over,
there's no longer a need to hide.

Come Dance with Me

Come dance with me in the night,
as flames rise up to darkened skies.
Come dance with me in the night,
like warriors from ages ago.
Come dance with me in the night,
till the embers of the sun begin to glow.
Come dance with me in the night,
without fears of tomorrow.

Broken and Bruised

Broken and bruised, I am, you see,
I've wasted my life, my eternity
on mindless work with no meaning to do.
All the while, what got me through was you.

Broken and bruised, not how I want to be.
What I was told is wrong, yet seems destined for me.
I chose my choices, so what's done is done.
Every day, we grow closer to the sun.

So I break away from my chains to catch a few rays,
then I melt away
as moments turn to days.
So soundly it went from autumn to spring,
but I know in my heart winter is closing in.

Unfinishable

So trying are days,
so trying are nights,
driving all alone,
driving out of sight.

Walk this world a soldier,
walk to your grave.
This is an unfinishable poem;
forever it shall stay.

Adjustment to Chaos

Simple light,
magnificent and bright,
shatters the world around us.

Broken dreams,
obscure and obscene,
awaken your nightly slumber.

Torn pages,
written by fools and sages—
you cannot read the right way.

Nothing is what it seems,
as nothing seems what it is.
Back and forth,
forth and back—
are you sure which way is up?

Nothing is everything,
but is everything enough?
This is your mind's adjustment to chaos.

Just Me

I'm sorry I don't act the way you want me to.
I'm sorry I don't fit the image you've drawn.
But I am me, and that's all I can be.
If that's not enough, there's no reason to stay.

Every word I speak,
every look I give,
is dissected and torn apart.
I wonder what's left of me
once you've picked me clean.

I am what I am—
a flawed design, perhaps, but mine.
I didn't think it was wrong to be this way,
to drift between happy and sad.
I'm just me; it's all I can be.
That's who I've always been,
right from the start.

Rotary

Dreams and aspirations,
leading to life's complications.
One way in and no way out—
the rotary of life to turn you roundabout.

And It Was

Take a walk into the darkness,
and slowly fall away.
Morning becomes night,
and still, we're feeling alright,
now standing at the foot of the bed where she lay.

Demon's Lament

Demon, demon, in my chair,
set me free—oh, this I dare.

Demon, demon, in my bed,
let me sleep or render me dead.

Demon, demon, in my eye,
show me the visions, show me the lies.

Demon, demon, in my head,
I will share with you
the voices of the living and the dead.

Cynical America

America, America, what has happened to thee?
Once tall and proud, now but a distant memory.
You must see with your eyes, through the politics and lies—
now sea to polluted sea.

Nothing left for good, mostly just the corrupt and misunderstood.
This is not my country, 'Tis of Thee.
America, America, once a land of the free,
so much taken for granted—you must realize
your freedom was never free.

The Walls Between

The distance between us grows;
the walls are built.
But it's my fault—
I feel this sickness inside.
But what does it show?

Folding Inward

Tears on the inside,
covering scars of the forgotten.
Tears on the outside,
washing away the pain.
Still, the memories remain.

Round and round—
this ain't no ride.
Down and down,
my spirit hides.

Folding in on myself—
a realization,
a dream.
Consequences be damned,
only shadows remain.

Difference

Mild complications,
words uttered from the doorstep.

YELL. SCREAM.
Nothing seems to matter—
a series of words strung together,
carrying no meaning.

Could it be that I've created the world's finest prison?
Encased in my mind,
trapped forever with endless thoughts,
none of them making any sense.

I'm looking for a way to escape,
yet the walls are so sturdy,
so thick that not a single ray of light glints through.

Where has the time gone?
What has been done
to create a place without escape?

Release me now. Free me.
Tear down the wall,
pluck me from this cage.
Show me the world
that my eyes have been too blind to see.

Then the voice says:
We have shown you these things.
It was you who built the wall,
and it is you who must tear it down,
brick by brick.

You are your own way
to salvation or damnation.
The choice has always been yours.

Disconnected

Another starless night,
caught somewhere between
reality and a dream.

I can't feel you—
have you stopped feeling me?

The switch was flipped,
and then I couldn't
find you.

Am I waiting
on a love that was not meant for me?

Pour your soul into me.
Bring me to the edge.
Will you stand
to watch me fall?

Burden

How long must I be strong?
Forever, they replied.
You have not earned weakness.

If the weight must fall,
from one, you shall inherit it.

This is your destiny.
This is the plan.

What does it mean to be me? Can I reply?
Am I a surrogate for aggression?
How do you find yourself
at the bottom of this hole?

Not tonight, they said.
SLEEP.

Outside In

Touch me, fuck me,
beat me—make me feel
something, anything.

Torment my fucking mind;
make me feel that I have been touched.

Drag me on the pavement,
rip me apart,
shred the flesh from my chest.

I am dead,
from the outside in.

Never Again

Maybe this time I can choose the way.
Maybe this time the pain will end.
Maybe this time it will be okay.
Never again will you treat me this way.

I can feel it getting closer to me,
but it's okay to stay away.
I know you're leering in the shadows
of my endless pain.

Through your constant insanity,
you never saw me for me.
Why would you think I'd stay,
always just another heartache away?

Maybe this time I can choose the way.
Maybe this time the pain will end.
Maybe this time it will be okay.
Never again will you treat me this way.

You keep on dragging me around
through shit you laid out.
Now that it's over,
I'll never be the same.

Maybe this time I can choose the way.
Maybe this time the pain will end.
Maybe this time it will be okay.
Never again will I let myself fade away.

Maybe this time I can choose the way.
Maybe this time the pain will end.
Maybe this time it will be okay.
Never again—because there will never be another day.

Never Knowing

Ahhhhh... I scream to the sky,
but yet I get no reply.
Can you not hear me?
Must I scream again?

You tell me I must play the fool,
and you the hero.
Well, I am not your child,
nor will I ever be.

How, in a time of need,
you all turned your back on me.
But the pain and anger—
you will never see.

I have risen above this place
to see the mountains far away.
I am your child no more;
I bet you wanted it that way.

They tell you to go for your dreams—
for what? So they can shoot them down.
I have bled for myself to survive,
and I have watched you all leave.

Don't think I don't understand it;
I had you figured out long before.
Never again must you call me your child,
because I am my own family now.

You might have borne me,
you might have raised me,
but don't ever tell me
that you were always there for me.

You want to know my anger,
you want to know my mistrust?
Well, look inside your own withering heart
and see that I am no more.

I would never give you the satisfaction
of never hearing me again.
When I have grown, you will know
where this pain and anger went.

PART 4:

The Precipice of Truth

Embers of Eden

Drunken mind of the innocent,
lost ship at sea.
The moon rises above Eden tonight.

Dance naked by the embers,
watch the world fade.

Twenty-one dollars and a paperback—
not much more to say.

Summer Slumber

Sedated dreams,
seaside breeze,
transient visions,
just waiting to be seen.

Tragic endings,
glorious beginnings—
all make up the essence
of this midsummer night's dream.

Ophidian

Slow motion,
a frozen moment in time,
forgotten memories,
left far behind.

Turning the pages
of your history,
knowing it's all there,
quarantined emotions,
because there's no need to share.

Shake down, shake down—
take off all that you wear.
So be the ophidian,
sliding into life.

Wild Creatures

There are wild creatures among us,
living, breathing, waiting
in the darkness of night.
They will drag you down,
grinding all the flesh and bone.

There are wild creatures among us,
dressed in suits and ties.
You know them, you see them—
you are them.
Now run and hide.

Barren Trees

There are days for the seasons,
and seasons for the year,
everything moving forward
in time as the drumbeat carries on.

How many more days will our seasons see?
How many more seasons will become years?
For some, that will be endless;
for others, the leaves of their final season
are beginning to fall.

When their trees become barren,
their last days will call for the final curtain.
As they approach the stage for their final ovation,
the lights will fade into darkness.
Only memories remain.

So long, farewell—your show is over,
and with that, we say goodbye.
Safe travels, and don't forget to write.

This, my dear and beloved friends,
is the end.

OverExposed

Exposed to the bittersweet taste of your life,
opened to a reality of such unmentionable fright.
If I left you alone in your dreams tonight,
could you honestly say it would be alright?

In a Life

Each road that we travel in this life
should be considered a new path to our destiny.

Each day we are awoken by the sun's illuminating light
should be another day closer to our dreams.

Each door we open
should be accounted as a new vision we have seen.

Every heart that we touch
should be another mark we have written in our history.

Every kiss that we give
is another chance for a heart to feel an endless love.

Every passionate moment that we have shared
must never be forgotten.

Forever in a Dream

Exposed to the harsh reality,
waking in the sand.
Dawn is upon us—
have we wasted the night,
or were we just wasted?

Lost moments drift between us.
Has it all been in vain,
trying to remember
what was said
and what was of dreams?

The moments we have lost
seem to be the best of this life.
To this, I must proclaim:
let us dream forever, my friend.

Whisper in the Wall

Let each moment carry on.
Let not a word be spoken.
In time, you will hear
the whispers in the wall.

For What Will Become

Lost friend among the ashes,
your voice will now be heard—
heard further than it could be
upon this fabricated soapbox.

Your words, left incomplete
on Tuesday morning,
I know as Sunday comes,
we will hear them complete.

For the birds shall scream it
above the clouds,
and the wind shall carry
your spirit home.

Now move forward
to your destiny.

Proclamation of Hell

Smoke fills the crowded room,
as flames rise around us.
We must first conquer
the fires of Hell
before we can proclaim our divinity.

In Time

Lost in a single moment of time,
for which we shall fall endlessly.
No more sour endings to the tragedy
where the Jester is beheaded before the court.

Nights of transient lust—
move on to your new home.
Feelings left untrusted
are better off left alone.

Trial and error to find the road home,
looking that way, not sure if you really want to go.
Leave what is.
Leave what should never be.

To give what you have
is never, but nearly, enough.
To give what you are
is to give all that you were.

Reasonable Sanity

Surely madness must have been too easy,
or else we would all be in a joyous state of mind.
We would all be at the grandest of parties,
indulging in the finest cup of wine.

And then the band would play,
as we laugh like children in the schoolyard.

Surely madness must have been too easy—
that's why they won't let us lose our minds.

Glimpse of Reality

The only times I cannot think
of something to write
are times when I am bogged down
in reality.

So I stare at blank pages
and hope it goes away.
After all, reality is what
I have made it to be—
making it only reality to me.

Free the Masses

City streets are always crowding;
there doesn't seem to be much room to move.
People gather around,
marching their way downtown.

Try to set them free—
from themselves or whatever it may be.
Just let go of what you have,
because when your time is up,
not much else will matter.

Fluid to Dust

I keep growing older
as the days pass by.
I keep on wondering
whether I'm dead or alive.

It seems every day
I keep moving down the road.
I guess there's no choice—
I have to keep growing old.

Recover

Can you see the light
as it shines down?
If you wait another minute,
it'll turn around.

It's all coming back now—
you'll see it all too clear.

Eight Days in September

Eight days in September—
not one that I can recall.

Eight days in September—
they were lived only to see you fall.

Maybe, had there been ten days in September,
we could've enjoyed them all.

A Little Bit More

The time is getting closer,
the lights are all going dim.
Somewhere in her shadows,
she sees visions of him.

Some things were made to be,
others just meant to fade away.
She knows he's out there somewhere;
he can't stand to see her this way.

It was never a storybook romance—
happy endings were far apart.
As she taps another vein,
it burns a hole right through his heart.

He can see it in her eyes,
and every time, he dies
just a little bit more.
With every vein she sticks,
she's always wanting
just a little bit more.

We can't break it,
we can't escape it,
because we all die
just a little bit more.
We can't stop it,
we can't drop it,
we're always wanting
just a little bit more.

Another vow is broken
as the barroom begins to clear.
With the lust in his eyes,
he knows his wife's not here.

Some things just can't be saved—
at times, it would be nice if they could.
That doesn't seem to matter;
he thinks he's done everything he should.

So he puts his ring away,
walks another girl out the door.
This time, it's gonna kill him—
because she's a junked-up whore.

His wife is home in bed,
trying to wait up
just a little bit more.
He's lying in a ditch,
wishing he got
just a little bit more.

We can't break it,
we can't escape it,
because we all die
just a little bit more.
We can't stop it,
we can't drop it,
we're always wanting
just a little bit more.

The days are getting colder—
it won't be long till they're through.
Got lost out on the highway,
searching for someone I once knew.

All the thoughts were crazy,
kept drifting further from it all.
Every day just went by;
I had no one left to call.

Out in the open world,
with so many places to go,
I found an empty road
with nobody left to show.

Could've stayed at home,
instead I had to roam
just a little bit more.
Now I'm still alone—
I went out searching for
just a little bit more.

We can't break it,
we can't escape it,
because we all die
just a little bit more.
We can't stop it,
we can't drop it,
we're always wanting
just a little bit more.

Eternal

Ink runs so easily from the paper,
yet lead only fades with time.
It would seem that while the written word
may live for a time,
that which is spoken and heard
is what becomes immortal.

PART 5:

Illuminations

A Note

These are not poems but fragments—fleeting sparks of thought and inspiration that have traveled with me through time. Each one offers a glimpse into the depths of my creative mind, capturing the places it has been and hinting at where it might yet go. I share them with you, raw and unfiltered, as moments of connection to the magical inner workings of the darkest corners of my mind.

Clarity and Truth

And from the light, a new day is born.

Eyes of perception shape the shallow mind.

Create only what you are willing to destroy, for if not, in the end, it will destroy you.

Life is a mental clinic where we've all checked in.

Ignorance is blind to that which it belongs.

Sometimes people can say a lot when they speak, but sometimes saying a lot means absolutely nothing at all.

Behind the broken mirror, there are stories to be told.

At points when we feel we are most alone, there is always a shadow to watch over us.

Is it eloquence or elegance?

Welcome to true consciousness; you are awake.

I wonder sometimes if I am going insane or just waking up to a bitter reality.

All the things that never made sense to me, I never needed to understand in the first place.

Let the walls collapse around me. Open the world.

Lead me beyond the shadows to a secret hideaway.

Northward bound to reach for the heavenly light above.

Yearning and Despair

Someone save me from this emptiness.

How can I find peace within myself when I cannot find myself?

Could you even hear my words after you stabbed me in the back?

Sometimes all I can do is never enough.

Lost in the wilderness of your wild heart.

As tears of sadness roll down my face, you stand to mock my pain.

No matter how lost I become in this life, I know someday my heart will find its way home.

Fell upon my stone to the grave I shall call home.

With waking light, the dawn has come, and soon I shall follow.

My walls are crumbling, and it has never felt better to be alive.

Somewhere, our souls are still together.

Live a life worth living; otherwise, you never lived at all.

Once my words meant something; now they are just empty spaces between breaths.

Existence and Mortality

Death's toll is paid when you cannot rest.

Death is just another chance for someone to make a buck.

Life is a picture book, and the pages change every day. Sooner or later, they will all be washed away.

The angels fly above me as the demons lurk below—each one waiting for the moment you let go.

Sweet songs of yesterday only seem to bring tears today.

A war with one's own mind will surely defeat that over the war with another.

When the rampart winds blow, I will only be dead inside.

The faster you run, the harder the fall. Never did the plummet feel so good.

Stupidity is a cure for some of life's more complicated problems.

Dreams and Imagination

At the contour of a dream, you inch ever closer to the edge of insanity.

Sensation, fascination of the unborn mind.

Shivers down my spine cause a pleasure so divine.

Somewhere, our souls are still together.

Tell me of the ghosts you have seen, and I shall tell you of those I've walked with.

Give up control and see where the ride takes you.

The world within is looking to find a way out.

Of all the words that I have written, your name has always been the sweetest.

Such a joyful game that we play.

Oh, are we here again? I thought it impossible to arrive at such a place twice in one lifetime.

Acknowledgements

Many have inspired the works you've just read, but one person, above all, took me on an emotional rollercoaster that ultimately brought these words to life. Some days were filled with joy, others felt like hell, but in the end, I'm left with a work of art and a life enriched by experience. Though I doubt you will ever read this— thank you.

Lynn Taylor and Alinar Den, your time and feedback on this draft were invaluable. I truly appreciate your insights.

Danna Mathais Steele, once again, you've created an incredible cover and layout design. Thank you for making my work shine!

And to all the wonderful people I've met on TikTok—your encouragement gave me the push I needed to bring this collection to the world. I'm deeply grateful. Thank you!

About the Author

Ron Shaw lives in New Hampshire, where he writes under the watchful eye—and occasional ambush—of his cat, Ophelia. With a master's degree in Public Administration from Norwich University, he balances a full-time tech career with his passion for storytelling. When not lost in the dark and twisted worlds of his novels, you can find him expanding his vintage NES collection or pondering life's mysteries with a healthy dose of sarcasm.

Where you can find me:

ronshawwrites.com
TikTok: @ronshaw603
Instagram: @ronshawwrites
Tome: @ronshaw603

Reviews are always welcome and appreciated!

www.ingramcontent.com/pod-product-compliance
Lightning Source LLC
Chambersburg PA
CBHW060339050426
42449CB00011B/2793